Spark

Virginija Bellasis

BookLeaf Publishing

India | USA | UK

Presentation by *BookLeaf Publishing*

Web: www.bookleafpub.com

E-mail: info@bookleafpub.com

ISBN: 9789360942359

First edition 2024

Missed goodbye

I didn't have a chance
To hold your hand.
It was so sudden...
And you left.
I'm standing here
Asking myself. Why?
I wish I had chance
To say last goodbye.

Pain of emptiness
Is ripping me apart.
I'm on my knees
Holding broken heart.
I wish I had,
More time with you
But now it's too late,
Nothing I can do.

Tears are rolling
Down to my face,
I'm trying to recall
All the good times.
Things I should have said
And didn't held back
But now it's too late
There is no come back.

Power in you

Sun inside you
Is shining bright.
Rain and clouds
Can dim that light.
Put your hand
On your chest
Feel the warmth
You are the best!

You are strong
You have power inside you!
Don't care about storms
No need to hide it!
Just go through it
Or fly above.
You have the power
You are strong enough!

Do not care
What people say.
They will judge you anyway.
Happy people
Will lift you up
That's all you need to know
Just don't give up!

Don't give up

You smile
But I can see sadness
In your eyes
The empty look
Hard to hide.
Talk to me, what's going on?
Let's switch the light
Inside you,back on!

You think you are weak?
You are not!
You think life is over?
It's not!
If you hit rock bottom
It's tough.
There is only one way
Is up!
Don't give up!
Don't give up!
Don't give up!

Put that crap down
It's time to move on.
You had fun
But this can't go on.

I'll be there with you
While you build yourself up.
Don't give up!
Don't give up!
Don't give up!

Tiny sparks of hope
Brighten up your eyes.
Now it's time to work
For a better life.
I'll be there with you
While you build yourself up.
Don't give up!
Don't give up!
Don't give up!

Heath

My wondering eyes
Keep following you
You look so good
In the Lycra ... who knew?
I can't focus on my exercise
You are distraction
That I don't mind.

Maybe it's you
Maybe it's heat
Maybe workout
Raised my heart beat
Every time
You catch me
Watching you
I can't stop blushing
I really like you.

Lifting too heavy weights,
Running too fast on treadmill.
All my body already aches,
I'll get your attention, I will.

I look desperate ISBN
And not very wise,

Why do I try get attention of man
That is older than me twice
Come on girl,
You can do better than that
Focus on your exercise.

First kiss

It was the moment
When we met for first time
Instant chemistry, magic
Lightening strike
Beautiful chaos happening
In the air
Soul's falling in love
Like no one else there

My toes were curling
When we had our first kiss
Bodies filled with emotions
Who wouldn't want to feel like this

You pulled me closer
Wrapped your arms around me
Looked in my eyes
And I could see
Soul full of love
Full of devotion
I was just melting
From all the emotion.

King

Exhausted and tired
After tough day
King comes back home
With not much to say

Quick kiss, jump in shower
Wash off the stress
Follow by dinner
And Queen in red dress

After the dinner
I'll be your desert
She said with a smile
And did little twirl

Queen rests hands
On Kings shoulders
She feels he's still little bit tense
She starts massaging him... gently
Until slowly he starts to chill

Next minute they were kissing
Her hands playing with him
Just playful and exciting
Tonight it's all about the King.

Christmas

Look around you
All the snow
Christmas here
Ho ho ho

Festive music and mince pies
I see joy in people's eyes
Frosty trees and chilli air
I see footprints here and there
Whose are they?
Oh I don't know?

But I see you all alone
Just bellow a mistletoe
I don't know you know or not
But I'm coming give you lot

Lots of kisses lots of love
And my heart that you can have

Chilling

Side to side
Changing positions
Getting nice tan
Looking delicious
Jumping in the water
Swimming to the bar
Ordering cocktail
Love it here so far

Sunny sunny sunny
Yummy yummy yummy
I love all the cocktails
Going in my tummy
Chocolate vanilla
Strawberry tequila
Having little mix
That's my headache next

Going to the beach
To catch up with friends
Palm trees
Coconut beach
Sun blue water
And maybe bit romance

Club

It's a busy club and very loud music
I'm dancing around not gonna loose it
Having a drink watching you come in
Didn't think nothing
But that's where we begin

My eyes are closed we are at the beach
I feel the ocean touching my feet
You holding me tight
Your strong arms around me
I love feel that feeling
Glad that you found me

It's late at night and we are both tipsy
Time to go back, but we start kissing.
My toes are curling
I'm melting inside
I don't want sun yet to rise.

Cheat

It's 3am I cannot sleep
Wasting my time
Thinking about you... cheat
It hurts a lot
You broke my heart
I'm looking forward
To a new start
I know you are mad
I'm kicking you out
Just shut the door
Behind you now

I feel your hate
Your love was fake
Now go away
It's very late
Just go away
Don't make a sound
Don't look behind
I won't cry loud.

I have big heart
My love was real
I give you chance
You didn't need

You had a chance
But trew it away
I'll be happy again
Wish you the same

I can feel it

I see you staying next door
Hope you are single, with mates
In our 5 plus star resort
I hope you are not checking out
Would be nice someday to hang out.

I can feel it, can feel it
You are dancing behind me
Come on closer, come closer
Wrap your arms around me
Feel my body, moving
Very slowly, slowly
Dance with me handsome
So I won't feel lonely, lonely

Chilling by the pool
Looking so cool
Hiding under shades
Sipping lemonade
Soothing my sore head
What a fun I had
See you bit later
Handsome alligator.

New beginnings

Popcorn is popping
Pop pop pop
Movie night in
Noooope!
I'm putting on my sexy dress
High heels, make up
Yes yes yes
Not staying home
Crying my eyes out
Celebrating freedom
I'm going out!

Nodding my head
To a great tune
My heart is jumping
I'm over the moon
I'm single now
Got all friends around
It's a new start
And I'm out

Harsh words

You say that you love me
But your harsh words
Weighing like stones deep inside me

You say it's because you want a reaction
But it's cruel way to be
My feelings does matter
I don't think you deserved me

Neither of us are perfect
But we still can be kind
Perhaps if we are so different
It's time to move apart
And leave this path behind

The one

We sat close enough
To feel our hearts beating in sync
To feel taking a breath
Love is written without ink

We awakened some incredible feeling
It was not butterflies
It was peace
We felt at home
But we haven't met before
It was nice feeling to feel

We couldn't look at each other's eyes
Because we were scare to admit
That we lit a fire
And it's not a small pit.

In your arms

Imagine how would it feel
Be desired, be loved.
Falling asleep at night,
In the arms of someone
You love.

His masculine perfume
Your mid sends a wild.
Makes you feel cosy
Makes inside you smile.

Skin touches skin,
Bodies get tangled up.
Wakes up with desire
To make love...

Do I like myself?

Wake up, have shower
Morning make up routine.
Rushing, got an hour
And tears
Starts coming down the face
Like a stream.

Make up is ruined,
She slumps back in the chair.
Sits with that uncomfortable feeling,
How did I get here?

Do I like myself?
She asked her reflection in the mirror.
I drink too much,
I eat too much.
I let myself go.
I mistreated myself,
No I don't like myself, no.

If I don't love me,
How can I expect,
Someone else to treat me
With more respect?

She pours the vine
Down in the sink.
Trows all chocolates,
Straight in the bin.

Goes back to the mirror,
Gives herself a smile.
Fixes the make up,
She took first step in the mile.

Morning

It was early morning
When sun rays woke her up.
She was drowsy and moaning
No she don't want to get up.

All warm and snug under the duvet
She closed her eyes
And imagined his hug
How would be nice in the morning
To wake up and make love

Passionate and steamy
To feel his body
On hers
She would kiss his neck slowly
Run fingers trough
His back
He tense up and move faster…
She could feel him
Coming inside
Pulsating, moaning
Then laughter
Good morning, did you had a good night?

She just smiled all wrapped up

Under the duvet
All hot and little steamed up
Her body needs little attention
And then she's will get up.

Love yourself first

Pay attention
How does he make you feel
Empowered and strong
So you could
Conquer the world?
Or weak, small, demanding
And have no worth?

Be true to yourself
And love yourself first
Make good decisions
So you can build
Solid foundations
To empower yourself
And you won't need validation
From no one else.

People treat you bad if you let them
Set the boundaries
Don't allow cross them.

To the reader

If I made you cry
Sorry that wasn't the aim.
Perhaps you had emotions
That was hidden inside
Wasn't meant to be touched?
And be left all alone?
But it was weighing you down
And it seems like it needed to go.

Try just sit with emotion
Let yourself feel what you feel
It's ok to be scared and uncomfortable
But that will help you heal.

When your tears will dry out
And you ready emotion to go
Just say:
I'm very grateful for this feeling
But now I'm letting you go.

And repeat hundred times
If you had to.
Until start feeling at peace
Let good emotions to rise up to
And let all the negative go.

Disaster first date

My knees are shaking
I have butterflies
I need a bathroom
Where can I hide

You slowly approaching
All looking nice
I'm so nervous
I want to run and hide

It's our first date
And it's a disaster
There is no chance
We'll see each other after
I spilled my drink
On your sexy top
I tripped over table
Landed like a flop

I think it's over
I'm panicking now
But he just smiles
Are you done now?
Let's go grab a coffee
I like you: he says.

I think you are funny
Let's get to know each other more

Island of sins

Please don't tell nobody,
We are getting tipsy tonight.
Tomorrow in the morning,
We are leaving to catch a flight.
Going to an island,
Where love stories begins
Lots of friends are coming
To the island of sins.

Semi naked bodies
Messing with my head
Dip your toes in the ocean
Let's the party start!
Move your body slowly
Drink your poison fast
Enjoy the emotions
While the summer lasts.

Chilling on the beach,
Inhaling fresh sea air.
Watching sun to rise
Found my love here.
This is magic island
Where love stories begin
Lots of friends

Found lovers
In the island of sins.